MW00468947

THE BOWL OF SAQI

THE BOWL OF SAQI
A Sufi Book of Days

Gender Inclusive Edition

Hazrat
Pir-o-Murshid
Inayat Khan

Edited and Annotated by
Netanel Miles-Yépez

Albion
Andalus
Boulder, Colorado

2012

*"The old shall be renewed,
and the new shall be made holy."*
— Rabbi Avraham Yitzhak Kook

Gender Inclusive Edition Copyright © 2012 Netanel Miles-Yépez
First edition. All rights reserved.

No part of this book may be reproduced or transmitted in any form or by any means, electronic or mechanical, including photocopy, recording, or any information storage or retrieval system, except for brief passages in connection with a critical review, without permission in writing from the publisher:

Albion-Andalus Inc.
P. O. Box 19852
Boulder, CO 80308
www.albionandalus.com

Design and composition by Albion-Andalus Inc.

Cover design by Albion-Andalus Inc.

"Rose-Heart and Wings" illustration © 2008 Netanel Miles-Yépez

Manufactured in the United States of America

ISBN-13: 978-0615611488
ISBN-10: 0615611486

CONTENTS

Editor's Preface

DESPITE THE SIMILARITY of sound and contexts between the culturally separate homonyms, *saqi* and *saki*, the title of this work is actually *The Bowl of Saqi*, and not, *A Bowl of Saki*, as some have mistakenly read it. Nevertheless, it is an interesting coincidence that the Japanese word for rice-wine fits so neatly into this title, especially as the Persian word of similar pronunciation actually means 'wine-bearer,' or 'one who pours the wine.' In a Sufi context, the *saqi* is the *murshid* or spiritual guide, who pours the wine of divine love from their own 'bowl' into the 'bowl' of the *murid*, the spiritual aspirant, leading to an intoxication with the Divine Beloved. But, on another level, the *saqi* is also the Spirit of Guidance itself, as the following poem from the personal notebooks of Hazrat Inayat Khan makes clear:

> *Your light which rises in my heart,*
> *May in the hearts of my murids shine.*
> *The juice that intoxicated me so,*
> *O Saqi, give my murids that wine.*
> *Surround my murids with Your beauty,*
> *Create in them Your harmony divine,*
> *Give them sympathy for one another*
> *May they forget the world's mine and thine.**

Another meaning implicit in this title has more to do with a Sufi's capacity to receive; for a Sufi must always have an empty 'bowl' with which to receive divine love from the Beloved. Thus, we must continually go through a process of self-emptying (often referred to in the aphorisms of this

---

* Adapted into modern English from the *Complete Works of Pir-o-Murshid Hazrat Inayat Khan, Original Texts: Sayings, Part II.*

collection) in order to become a proper vessel of love. Sometimes it is the pouring-out of self-conceit, and sometimes it is simply the sharing of love, the out-pouring of love from 'bowl to bowl,' as it were.

The title, *The Bowl of Saqi*, was actually chosen by the disciples of Pir-o-Murshid (though he had used the phrase in his lectures) when this collection was first published in England in late 1921 or early 1922.* Contained in it were 366 aphorisms which might be used as meditations for each day of the year. Apparently these had been selected from the teachings of the master, many coming directly from his lectures, while still others came from his personal notebooks. In this edition, I have edited the originals for clarity and made them gender inclusive (rather than using the masculine personal pronoun in an inclusive sense, as was the convention in Pir-o-Murshid's day). I have also annotated the aphorisms in places where I thought it necessary to explain non-English vocabulary and to note important days on the calendar of Inayati Sufis.

It is my hope that you will enjoy these aphorisms and use them daily to re-attune to the blessed presence of the Beloved.

Netanel Miles-Yépez, Boulder, Colorado,

March 2nd, 2012, the day on which we read . . .

The priest gives a benediction from the church;
The branches of the tree in bending
Give a blessing from God.

---

* In December 1921, the new book was announced in the quarterly publication, *Sufism*, with the words: "a collection of some of the most striking and arresting sayings of Pir-o-Murshid, arranged in the form of a daily textbook." *Complete Works of Pir-o-Murshid Hazrat Inayat Khan, Original Texts: Sayings, Part II.*

JANUARY

JANUARY 1

As water in a fountain flows as one stream
And falls in many drops, divided by time and space,
So are the revelations of the one stream of truth.

JANUARY 2

All names and forms
Are garments and covers
Under which the one life is hidden.

JANUARY 3

Truth without a veil
Is always uninteresting to the human mind.

JANUARY 4

When you stand

With your back to the Sun,

Your shadow is before you;

But when you turn and face the Sun,

Your shadow falls behind you.

JANUARY 5

No one has seen God and lived.

To see God, we must be non-existent.

JANUARY 6

The truth cannot be spoken;

That which can be spoken is not the truth.

JANUARY 7

The only power for the mystic
Is the power of love.

JANUARY 8

If people but knew their *own* religion,
How tolerant they would become,
And how free from any grudge
Against the religion of others.

JANUARY 9

The real meaning of crucifixion

Is to crucify the false self

That the true Self may arise.*

As long as the false self is not crucified,

The true Self is not realized.

JANUARY 10

An ideal is beyond explanation.

To analyze God is to dethrone God.

JANUARY 11

Where the flame of love rises,

The knowledge of God unfolds of itself.

---

* The Latin, *crucifigere*, literally means, 'to attach to a cross,' referring to the Roman punishment of nailing persons (most notably, Jesus of Nazareth) to wooden beams; but we might also note from Hazrat Inayat Khan's teaching that sacrifice is the axis between us and God.

JANUARY 12

Peace is perfected activity;

That is perfect which is complete in all its aspects,

Balanced in each direction,

And under complete control of the will.

JANUARY 13

Do not limit God to your virtue.

God is beyond your virtues, pious ones!

JANUARY 14

One's inclination

Is the root of the tree

Of one's own life.

JANUARY 15

Yes, teach your principles of good,
But do not think to limit God within them.
The goodness of each person
Is peculiar to that being.

JANUARY 16

To learn to adopt the standard of God,
And to cease to wish to make the world conform
To one's own standard of good
Is the chief lesson of religion.

JANUARY 17

Thought
Draws the line of fate.

JANUARY 18

Mistaken belief alone misleads;

Single-mindedness always leads to the goal.

JANUARY 19

A sovereign

Is ever a sovereign,

Whether crowned with a jeweled crown,

Or clad in a beggar's garb.

JANUARY 20

To treat everyone

As a shrine of God

Is to fulfill all religion.

JANUARY 21

The wise

Keep the balance

Between love and power;

Keeping the love in one's nature

Ever increasing and expanding,

And at the same time,

Strengthening the will

So that the heart

May not easily

Be broken.

JANUARY 22

Failure comes

When will surrenders to reason.

JANUARY 23

Success comes
When reason, the storehouse of experience,
Surrenders to will.

JANUARY 24

There is an answer to every call;
Those who call on God, to them God comes.

JANUARY 25

One who thinks
Against their own desire,
Is their own enemy.

JANUARY 26

The brain speaks through words;
The heart in the glance of the eyes;
And the soul through a radiance
That charges the atmosphere,
Magnetizing all.

JANUARY 27

Love is the merchandise
Which all the world demands;
If you store it in your heart,
Every soul will become your customer.

JANUARY 28

Sincerity is the jewel
That forms in the shell of the heart.

JANUARY 29

Self-pity
Is the worst poverty;
It overwhelms one until one sees nothing
But illness, trouble and pain.

JANUARY 30

The heart is not living
Until it has experienced pain.

JANUARY 31

The pleasures of life are blinding;
It is love alone that clears the rust from the heart,
The mirror of the soul.

FEBRUARY

FEBRUARY 1

The pain of love
Is the dynamite that breaks the heart,
Even if it be as hard as rock.

FEBRUARY 2

Our virtues are made of love,
And our sins are caused by a lack of it.

FEBRUARY 3

Love is the essence of all
Religion, mysticism and philosophy.

FEBRUARY 4

The fire of devotion

Purifies the heart of the devotee,

And leads to spiritual freedom.

FEBRUARY 5[*]

Mysticism

Without devotion

Is like uncooked food;

It can never be assimilated.

FEBRUARY 6

One who stores evil in the heart

Cannot see beauty.

---

[*] The *urs* (death anniversary) of Hazrat Pir-o-Murshid Inayat Khan. He died at 8:20 A.M., in Delhi, India, 1927. Called *Visalat* (return, reconnection) among Inayati Sufis.

FEBRUARY 7

The wise one,

By studying nature,

Enters into unity through variety,

And realizes the personality of God

By sacrificing their own.

FEBRUARY 8

Love manifests

Toward those whom we like—

As love;

Toward those whom we do not like—

As forgiveness.

FEBRUARY 9

Love brought us

From the world of unity

To that of variety,

And the same force can take us back

To the world of unity

From the world of variety.

FEBRUARY 10

Whoever knows the mystery of vibrations,

Indeed, knows all things.

FEBRUARY 11

One who arrives

At the state of indifference

Without experiencing interest in life is incomplete

And apt to be tempted by interest at any moment;

But one who arrives at the state of indifference

By going *through* interest, really attains

To the blessed state.

FEBRUARY 12

Wisdom is greater and more difficult to attain

Than intellect, piety or spirituality.

FEBRUARY 13

Wisdom is intelligence in its pure essence,

Which is not necessarily dependent upon

The knowledge of names and forms.

FEBRUARY 14

We form our future by our actions;

Every good or bad action spreads its vibrations,

And becomes known throughout the Universe.

FEBRUARY 15

The Universe is like a dome;

It vibrates to that which you say in it,

And answers the same back to you;

So also is the law of action;

We reap what we sow.

FEBRUARY 16

We are always

Searching for God, afar off,

When all the while, God is nearer to us

Than our own soul.

FEBRUARY 17

Concentration and contemplation are great things;
But no contemplation is greater than the life
We have about us every day.

FEBRUARY 18

One who expects
To change the world
Will be disappointed;
One must change one's own view.
When this is done,
Then tolerance will come,
Forgiveness will come,
And there will be nothing
One cannot bear.

FEBRUARY 19

To renounce

What we cannot gain

Is not true renunciation—

It is weakness.

FEBRUARY 20

The religion of each

Is the attainment of the soul's desire;

When one is on the path of that attainment,

One is religious;

When one is off that path,

One is impious.

FEBRUARY 21

The reformer

Comes to plough the ground;

The prophet

Comes to sow the seed;

And the priest

Comes to reap the harvest.

FEBRUARY 22

Life is an opportunity

Given to satisfy the hunger and thirst of the soul.

FEBRUARY 23

Truth alone can succeed;

Falsehood is a waste of time

And a loss of energy.

FEBRUARY 24

Do not fear God,
But consciously regard
God's pleasure and displeasure.

FEBRUARY 25

One who fails oneself, fails all;
One who conquers the self, wins all.

FEBRUARY 26

As we rise above passion,
We begin to know love.

FEBRUARY 27

Believe in God
With childlike faith;
For simplicity with intelligence
Is the sign of the holy ones.

FEBRUARY 28

One who can live up to one's own ideal
Is the sovereign of life;
One who cannot is life's slave.

FEBRUARY 29

Every moment of our life
Is an invaluable opportunity.

MARCH

MARCH 1

Nature speaks louder
Than the call from the *minaret*.*

MARCH 2

The priest gives a benediction from the church;
The branches of the tree in bending
Give a blessing from God.

---

* A *minaret* is an Islamic architectural structure, usually a tall spire from which the call to prayer *(aza'an)* is given by the *muezzin*.

25

MARCH 3

The soul brings its light from Heaven;
The mind acquires its knowledge from Earth.
Therefore, when the soul believes readily,
The mind may still doubt.

MARCH 4

Those who throw dust at the Sun,
The dust falls in their eyes.

MARCH 5

We create
Our own disharmony.

MARCH 6

The real book of God
Is in the human heart;
When it is frozen with bitterness or hatred,
The doors of the shrine are closed;
The light is hidden.

MARCH 7

It is a false love
That does not uproot one's claim of "I";
The first and last lesson of love is,
"I am not."

MARCH 8

You cannot be both horse and rider
At the same time.

MARCH 9

It is more important
To know the truth about one's self
Than to try to find out the truth
Of Heaven and Hell.

MARCH 10

Everyone's pursuit
Is according to their own evolution.

MARCH 11

One sees what one sees;
Beyond it, one cannot see.

MARCH 12

The source of truth
Is within the human being;
The human being is the object of its realization.

MARCH 13

As life unfolds itself to the human being,
The first lesson one learns is humility.

MARCH 14

God is truth;
And truth is God.

MARCH 15

Until one loses oneself in the vision of God,
One cannot be said to live, really.

MARCH 16

At every step of evolution,
The realization of God changes.

MARCH 17

Truly, one is victorious
Who has conquered the self.

MARCH 18

Prayer is the greatest virtue,
The only way of being free from all sin.

MARCH 19

It is the sincere devotee
Who knows best how to humble the self
Before God.

MARCH 20

It is wise to see all things,
And yet to turn our eyes from
All that should be overlooked.

MARCH 21

Our soul is blessed
With the impression of the glory of God
Whenever our lips praise God.

MARCH 22

There is one teacher, God alone;
We are all God's pupils.

MARCH 23

All earthly knowledge
Is as a cloud covering the Sun.

MARCH 24

The first sign of the realization of truth
Is tolerance.

MARCH 25

One who is filled
With the knowledge of names and forms
Has no capacity for the knowledge of God.

MARCH 26

One is closer to God
Than the fish are to the ocean.

MARCH 27

We start our lives
Trying to be teachers;
It is very hard to learn to be a pupil.

MARCH 28

Until the heart is empty,
It cannot receive the knowledge of God.

MARCH 29

According to one's evolution,
One knows truth.

MARCH 30

We can never sufficiently humble our limited self
Before limitless perfection.

MARCH 31

Even to utter the name of God
Is a blessing that can fill the soul
With light and joy and happiness
As nothing else can do.

APRIL

APRIL 1

When one praises the beauty of God,
The soul is filled with bliss.

APRIL 2

Sympathy is the root of religion;
As long as the spirit of sympathy
Is living in your heart,
You have the light of religion.

APRIL 3

Life is a misery for one
Absorbed only in the self.

APRIL 4

To give sympathy is sovereignty,
To desire it from others is captivity.

APRIL 5

God speaks to the ears of every heart,
But it is not every heart that hears God.

APRIL 6

As one can see when the eyes are open,
So one can understand when the heart is open.

APRIL 7

Being transparent to the self
Is the recognition of God.

APRIL 8

As the light of the Sun helps the plant to grow,
So the Divine Spirit helps the soul
Toward its perfection.

APRIL 9

Things are worthwhile when we seek them,
Only then do we know their value.

APRIL 10

When a one looks at the ocean,
One can only see that part of it
That comes within one's range of vision;
So it is with the truth.

APRIL 11

It does not matter in what way a person
Offers respect and reverence
To the deity one worships,
It matters only how sincere
One is in one's offering.

APRIL 12

The ideal of God
Is a bridge connecting
The limited life with the unlimited;
Whosoever travels over this bridge
Passes safely from the limited to the unlimited life.

APRIL 13

One who wants to understand
Will understand.

APRIL 14

We are the picture
Of the reflection of our imagination;
We are as large or as small as we think ourselves.

APRIL 15

The great teachers of Humanity
Become streams of love.

APRIL 16

"God is love"—
Three words which open up an unending realm
For the thinker who desires to probe the depths
Of the secret of life.

APRIL 17

It is the surface of the sea
That makes waves and roaring breakers;
The depth is silent.

APRIL 18

Our success or failure
Depends upon the harmony or disharmony
Of our individual will
With the Divine Will.

APRIL 19

The wave realizes, "I am the sea,"
And by falling into the sea
Prostrates itself to its God.

APRIL 20

The secret of happiness
Is hidden under the cover
Of spiritual knowledge.

APRIL 21

The soul is first born
Into the false self,
And it is blind;
In the true Self,
The soul opens its eyes.

APRIL 22

To learn the lesson of how to live
Is more important than any psychic
Or occult knowledge.

APRIL 23

Knowledge without love
Is lifeless.

APRIL 24

The aim of the mystic
Is to keep near to the idea of unity
And to find out where we unite.

APRIL 25

Sleep is comfortable,
But awakening is interesting.

APRIL 26

Every moment
Has its special message.

APRIL 27

To make God a reality
Is the real object of worship.

APRIL 28

Every passion,
Every emotion has
Its effect upon the mind,
And every change of mind,
However slight, has its effect upon the body.

APRIL 29

When souls meet one another,
What truth they can exchange!
It is uttered in silence,
Yet always reaches its goal.

APRIL 30

All gains,
Material, spiritual, moral or mystical,
Are in answer to one's own character.

MAY

MAY 1

You can have
All good things—
Wealth, friends, kindness,
Love to give and love to receive—
Once you have learned not to be blinded by them,
Learned to escape from disappointment
And repugnance at the idea that things are not
As you want them to be.

MAY 2

The truth need not be veiled,
For it veils itself from the eyes of the ignorant.

MAY 3

No one should allow their mind to be a vehicle

For others to use;

One who does not direct their own mind

Lacks mastery.

MAY 4

Rest of mind

Is as necessary

As rest of body,

And yet we always

Keep the former in action.

MAY 5

Those who have given deep thought to the world

Are those who have controlled the activity

Of their minds.

MAY 6

Unity in realization
Is far greater than unity in variety.

MAY 7

The afterlife
Is like a gramophone;
One's mind brings the records;
If they are harsh, the instrument
Produces harsh notes,
If beautiful,
Then it will sing beautiful songs.
It will produce the same records
That it has experienced
In this life.

MAY 8

One who depends
Upon the eyes for sight,
The ears for hearing, and the mouth for speech,
That one is still dead.

MAY 9

We cover our spirit under our body,
Our light under a bushel;
We never allow the spirit to become
Conscious of itself.

MAY 10

When we
Devote ourselves
To the thought of God,
All illumination and revelation is ours.

MAY 11

God communication

Is the best communication

That true spiritualism can teach us.*

MAY 12

The mystic desires

What Omar Khayyam calls wine,**

The wine of Christ,***

Which after drinking, no one will ever thirst.

---

* In Pir-o-Murshid's time, as in our own, there was much fascination with the occult and psychic phenomena, especially communication with disembodied spirits, often called "spiritualism."

** Omar Khayyám (1048–1131) was a Persian poet, author of the *Rubaiyat* (quatrains). Wine is a frequent topic in this work, and since whether Omar Khayyám was a Sufi or not is in dispute, it is likewise unclear whether wine is meant literally or metaphorically. Sufis are usually inclined to consider him a Sufi, and since the *Rubaiyat* was probably the most generally known work using this symbolism in Pir-o-Murshid's time, he could use the example of Omar Khayyám much in the same way as one can refer to Rumi today. So wine in this context is the love of God.

*** The "wine of Christ" is a reference to the wine of the Last Supper, a symbol of the blood of Christ, Christ's salvific compassion or love.

MAY 13

Our limited self is a wall
Separating us from the Self of God.

MAY 14

The wisdom and justice of God
Are within us, and yet, they are far away,
Hidden by the veil of the limited self.

MAY 15

One who is looking for a reward
Is smaller than the reward;
One who has renounced a thing
Has risen above it.

MAY 16

The poverty
Of one who has renounced is a treasure
When compared with the riches of one
Who holds them fast.

MAY 17

Love for God is the expansion of the heart,
And all actions that come from the lover of God
Are virtues: they cannot be otherwise.

MAY 18

God is the ideal
That raises Humanity
To the utmost of perfection.

MAY 19

One is wise

Who treats an acquaintance as a friend,

And one is foolish

Who treats a friend as an acquaintance,

And one is impossible

Who treats friends and acquaintances as strangers;

You cannot help that person.

MAY 20

Insight into life is the real religion,

That alone can help one to understand life.

MAY 21

The realization

That the whole of life must be "give and take"

Is the realization of the spiritual truth

And the fact of true democracy;

Not until this spirit is formed in the individual

Can the whole world be elevated

To the higher grade.

MAY 22

The perfect life

Is following one's own ideal,

Not in checking those of others;

Leave everyone to follow their own ideal.

MAY 23

Everyone's desire
Is according to their evolution;
That which one is ready for,
Is the desirable thing for them.

MAY 24

Discussion is for those who say,
"What I say is right, and what you say is wrong."
A sage never says a thing,
Hence there is no discussion.

MAY 25

Tolerance
Does not come by learning, but by insight,
By understanding that each person
Should be allowed to travel along the path
Which is suited to their temperament.

MAY 26

So long as one has a longing
To obtain any particular object,
One cannot go further than that object.

MAY 27

Every person's path is for themselves;
Let them accomplish their own desires,
That they may thus be able to rise above them
To the eternal goal.

MAY 28

The control of self

Means the control of everything.

MAY 29

"God is love"—*

When love is awakened in the heart,

God is awakened there.

MAY 30

All the disharmony of the world

Caused by religious differences

Is the result of one's failure to understand

That religion is one, truth is one, God is one;

How can there be two religions?

---

* *The New Testament,* I John 4: 8.

MAY 31

The use of friendship for a selfish motive
Is like mixing bitter poison with a sweet rose syrup.

JUNE

JUNE 1

One's bodily appetites
Take one away from the heart's desire;
The heart's desires keep one away
From the abode of the soul.

JUNE 2

Words are but the shadows
Of thoughts and feelings.

JUNE 3

The more elevated the soul,
The broader is the outlook.

JUNE 4

The secret of a friend
Should be kept as one's own;
The fault of a friend
Should be hidden as one's own.

JUNE 5

Forbearance, patience and tolerance
Are the only conditions that keep
Two individual hearts united.

JUNE 6

We blame others
For our sorrows and misfortunes,
Not perceiving that we ourselves
Are creators of our world.

JUNE 7

Nobody appears inferior to us
When our heart is kindled with kindness
And our eyes are open to the vision of God.

JUNE 8

Selfishness
Keeps one blind through life.

JUNE 9

The final victory
In the battle of life for every soul
Is when one has risen above the things
Which once one valued most.

JUNE 10

When power leads and wisdom follows,
The face of wisdom is veiled and it stumbles;
But when wisdom leads and power follows,
They arrive safely at their destination.

JUNE 11

One's whole conduct in life
Depends upon what one holds in one's thought.

JUNE 12

One who can be detached enough
To keep one's eyes open to all those
Whom circumstances have placed about one,
And to see in what way one can be of help to them,
It is that one who becomes rich—inheriting
The sovereignty of God.

JUNE 13

True justice cannot be perceived
Until the veil of selfishness has been
Removed from the eyes.

JUNE 14

Our thoughts have prepared us
For the happiness or unhappiness we experience.

JUNE 15

Love is the best means
Of making the heart capable
Of reflecting the soul power;
Love in the sense of pain
Rather than of pleasure.
Every blow opens a door
From whence the soul power
Comes forth.

JUNE 16

Every experience
Of the physical, astral or mental plane
Is just a dream before the soul.

JUNE 17

The fire of devotion
Purifies the heart of the devotee
And leads unto spiritual freedom.

JUNE 18

When love's fire produces its flame,
It illuminates like a torch the devotee's path in life,
And all darkness vanishes.

JUNE 19

It is mistrust that misleads;

Sincerity always leads straight to the goal.

JUNE 20

Love lies in service;

Only that which is done not for fame or name,

Not for the appreciation or thanks

Of those for whom it is done,

Is love's service.

JUNE 21

The soul is all light;

Darkness is caused by the deadness of the heart;

Pain makes it alive.

JUNE 22

The quality of forgiveness
That burns all things except beauty
Is the quality of love.

JUNE 23

Each of us
Composes the music of our own life;
If we injure another, we break the harmony
And there is discord in the melody of our life.

JUNE 24

One who with sincerity
Seeks a real purpose in life
Is also sought by that purpose.

JUNE 25

Through motion and change,

This life becomes intelligible;

We live a life of change, but it is constancy we seek.

It is this innate desire of the soul

That leads the human being to God.

JUNE 26

Every one of us has a definite vocation,

And our vocation is the light

That illuminates our life.

The one who disregards

One's own vocation

Is a lamp unlit.

JUNE 27

The heart sleeps
Until it is awakened to life by a blow.
It is as a rock, and the hidden fire flashes out
When struck by another rock.

JUNE 28

The awakened heart says,
"I must give; I must not demand."
Thus it enters a state that
Leads to a constant happiness.

JUNE 29

The Worlds are held together
By the heat of the Sun;
Each of us are atoms
Held by the eternal Sun of God.
Within us is the same central power we call
The light, or the love of God;
By it we hold together
The human beings
Within our sphere,
Or lacking it, *we*
Let them fall.

JUNE 30

When one dives within,
One finds that one's real self is above
The perpetual motion of the Universe.

JULY

JULY 1

Our pride and satisfaction in what we know
Limits the scope of our vision.

JULY 2

One must first create peace in oneself
If one desires to see peace in the world;
For lacking peace within,
No effort can bring any result.

JULY 3

The knowledge of self
Is the essential knowledge.
It gives the knowledge of Humanity;
In the understanding of the human being
Lies that understanding of Nature
Which reveals the law of creation.

JULY 4

While some blame another for causing them harm,
The wise first take themselves to task.

JULY 5[*]

Whatever their faith,

The wise have always

Been able to meet one another

Beyond those boundaries of external forms

And conventions that are natural

And necessary to human life,

But which nonetheless separate Humanity.

JULY 6

It is the Message

That proves the Messenger,

Not the claim.

---

[*] The birthday of Hazrat Pir-o-Murshid Inayat-Allah Khan, 11:35 P.M., Baroda (Vadodara), Gujarat, India, 1882. Called *Viladat* (birthday) among Inayati Sufis.

JULY 7

Every soul has a definite task,
And the fulfillment of each individual purpose
Can alone lead one aright;
Illumination comes to one
Through the medium
Of one's own talent.

JULY 8

While some judge others
From their own moral standpoint,
The wise also look from the point of view
Of the other.

JULY 9

While some rejoice over their own rise,
And sorrow over their own fall,
The wise take both as the
Natural consequences of life.

JULY 10

It is the lover of God
Whose heart is filled with devotion,
Who can commune with God,
Not one who makes an effort with the intellect
To analyze God.

JULY 11

Do not bemoan the past,
Do not worry about the future,
But try to make the best of today.

JULY 12

One who can quicken the feeling of another
To joy or to gratitude,
Adds to one's own life.

JULY 13

Praise cannot exist without blame;
It has no existence without its opposite.

JULY 14

Riches and power may vanish
Because they are outside ourselves;
Only that which is within can we call our own.

JULY 15

The world is evolving
From imperfection toward perfection—
It needs all love and sympathy.
Great tenderness and watchfulness is required
From each one of us.

JULY 16

The heart of every person,
Both good and bad, is the abode of God,
And care should be taken never to wound anyone
By word or act.

JULY 17

We should be careful
To take away from ourselves any thorns
That prick us in the personality of others.

JULY 18

There is a light within every soul;
It only needs the clouds that overshadow it
To be broken for it to beam forth.

JULY 19

The soul's true happiness
Lies in experiencing the inner joy,
And it will never be fully satisfied
With outer, *seeming* pleasures.
Its connection is with God,
And nothing short of perfection
Will ever satisfy it.

JULY 20

Every blow in life pierces the heart
And awakens our feelings
To sympathize with others;
And every swing of comfort lulls us to sleep
And we become unaware of all.

JULY 21

A study of life
Is the greatest of all religions,
And there is no greater or more interesting study.

JULY 22

We can learn virtue
From the greatest sinners
If we consider them teachers.

JULY 23

Warmth melts, while cold freezes.

A drop of ice in a warm place

Spreads and covers a large space,

Whereas a drop of water in a cold place

Freezes and becomes limited.

Repentance has the effect of spreading

A drop in a warm sphere,

Causing the heart to expand and become Universal,

While the hardening of the heart

Brings limitations.

JULY 24

There should be

A balance in all our actions—

To be either extreme or lukewarm is equally bad.

JULY 25

Our spirit

Is the real part of us,

The body but its garment.

One should not find peace

At the tailor's because the coat comes from there;

Neither can the spirit obtain true happiness

From the earth just because its body

Belongs to earth.

JULY 26

Every purpose

Has a birth and death;

Therefore, God is beyond purpose.

JULY 27

Belief and disbelief
Have divided Humankind into many sects,
Blinding our eyes to the vision of the oneness
Of all life.

JULY 28

Spirit can only love spirit;
In loving form, it deludes itself.

JULY 29

To love is one thing;
To understand is another.
One who loves is a devotee,
But one who understands is a friend.

JULY 30

Among a million believers in God
There is scarcely one who makes God a reality.

JULY 31

The soul feels suffocated
When the doors of the heart are closed.

AUGUST

AUGUST 1

Understanding
Makes the trouble of life
Lighter to bear.

AUGUST 2

The same herb
Planted in different atmospheric conditions
Will vary in form accordingly,
But will retain its characteristics.

AUGUST 3

Think before envying
The position of someone else—
With what difficulty have they arrived at it?

AUGUST 4

Life is what it is,

You cannot change it;

But you can always change yourself.

AUGUST 5

Life is a continual

Series of experiences,

One leading to the other

Until the soul arrives at its destination.

AUGUST 6

External life

Is the shadow of the inner Reality.

AUGUST 7

At the cost of one failure,
The wise learn a lesson for their whole life.

AUGUST 8

The more you evolve spiritually,
The further you pass from
The understanding of anyone.

AUGUST 9

One word
Can be more precious
Than all the treasures of earth.

AUGUST 10

Narrowness is primitiveness;
It is the breadth of heart that proves evolution.

AUGUST 11

It is simpler
To find a way to Heaven
Than to find a way on Earth.

AUGUST 12

It is God
Who, by our hands,
Designs and carries out
God's intended plans in Nature.

AUGUST 13

The lover of Nature
Is the true worshipper of God.

AUGUST 14

In the country,
You see the glory of God;
In the city, you glorify God's name.

AUGUST 15

The pain of life
Is the price paid
For the quickening of the heart.

AUGUST 16

Words that enlighten the soul
Are more precious than jewels.

AUGUST 17

Love is
The current coin
Of all peoples in all periods.

AUGUST 18

Do not take the example of another
As an excuse for your own wrong-doing.

AUGUST 19

Overlook the fault of another
But do not partake of it yourself,
Even in the smallest degree.

AUGUST 20

Cleverness and complexity
Are not necessarily wisdom.

AUGUST 21

The whole world's treasure
Is too small a price to pay for a word
That kindles the soul.

AUGUST 22

One is living whose sympathy is awake,
And one is dead, whose heart is asleep.

AUGUST 23

By our thoughts
We have prepared for ourselves
The happiness or unhappiness we experience.

AUGUST 24

Put your trust in God for support
And see God's hidden hand working
Through all sources.

AUGUST 25

Faith is the ABC

Of the realization of God.

This faith begins by prayer.

AUGUST 26

Passion is the smoke,

And emotion is the glow of love's fire.

Unselfishness is the flame that illuminates the path.

AUGUST 27

The soul of Christ*

Is the light of the Universe.

---

* Note that he has not said "Jesus" here, but "Christ," which is to say, the 'anointed one.'

AUGUST 28

Death is a tax

The soul has to pay

For having had a name and form.

AUGUST 29

A pure life

And a clean conscience

Are as two wings attached to the soul.

AUGUST 30

The giver is

Greater than the gift.

AUGUST 31

One who has spent, has used;
One who has collected, has lost;
But one who has given,
Has saved the treasure forever.

SEPTEMBER

SEPTEMBER 1

Joy and sorrow

Both are for each other.

If it were not for joy, sorrow could not be;

And if it were not for sorrow,

Joy could not be experienced.

SEPTEMBER 2

Self-pity is the cause

Of all life's grievances.

SEPTEMBER 3

How can the unlimited be limited?

All that seems limited is in its depth

Beyond all limitations.

SEPTEMBER 4

Pleasure blocks,
But pain clears the way of inspiration.

SEPTEMBER 5

There is no source of happiness
Other than that in the heart of Humanity.

SEPTEMBER 6

Happy is one
Who does good to others;
Miserable is one
Who expects good from others.

SEPTEMBER 7

One virtue is more powerful
Than a thousand vices.

SEPTEMBER 8

The soul is either raised or cast down
By the power of its own thought, speech and action.

SEPTEMBER 9

Love is the Divine Mother's arms;
When those arms are spread,
Every soul falls into them.

SEPTEMBER 10

It is the fruit
That makes the tree bow low.

SEPTEMBER 11

In order to learn forgiveness,
One must first learn tolerance.

SEPTEMBER 12

The first step
Toward forgiveness
Is to forget.

SEPTEMBER 13[*]

The only way to live

In the midst of inharmonious influences

Is to strengthen the will-power

And endure all things,

Yet keeping fineness of character

And nobility of manner

Together with an ever-living heart full of love.

SEPTEMBER 14

Devotion to a spiritual teacher

Is not for the sake of the teacher, it is for God.

---

[*] On September 13th, 1910, Hazrat Pir-o-Murshid Inayat Khan departed from India at the direction of his *murshid* to come to the West. This is known as *Hejirat* among Inayati Sufis.

SEPTEMBER 15

To become cold

From the coldness of the world is weakness;

To become broken by the hardness of the world

Is feebleness;

But to live in the world, and yet, to keep above it,

Is like walking on the water.

SEPTEMBER 16

God alone

Deserves all love,

And the freedom of love

Is in giving it to God.

SEPTEMBER 17

Love has the power

To open the door of eternal life.

SEPTEMBER 18

Love has its limitations
When directed toward limited beings,
But love directed to God has no limitations.

SEPTEMBER 19

The teacher, however great,
Can never give their knowledge to the pupil;
The pupil must create their own knowledge.

SEPTEMBER 20

One thing is true:
Although the teacher
Cannot give the knowledge,
The teacher can kindle the light
If the oil is in the lamp.

SEPTEMBER 21

Willpower

Is the keynote of mastery,

And asceticism is the development of will-power.

SEPTEMBER 22

Real generosity

Is an unfailing sign of spirituality.

SEPTEMBER 23

There are two kinds

Of generosity—the real and the shadow;

The former is prompted by love,

The latter by vanity.

SEPTEMBER 24

It is better to pay
Than to receive from the vain,
For such favors demand ten times their cost.

SEPTEMBER 25

The sovereignty of Heaven
Is in the hearts of those who realize God.

SEPTEMBER 26

In order to relieve
The hunger of others,
We must forget our own hunger.

SEPTEMBER 27

It is when one has lost
The idea of separateness,
And feels a oneness with all creation,
That the eyes are opened
And one sees the cause of all things.

SEPTEMBER 28

To fall beneath one's ideal
Is to lose one's share of life.

SEPTEMBER 29

The wise of all ages have taught
That it is knowledge of the Divine Being
That is life and the only Reality.

SEPTEMBER 30

When the stream of love flows in its full strength,

It purifies all that stands in its way,

As the Ganges—*

According to the teaching of the ancients—

Purifies all those who plunge into its sacred waters.

---

* The Ganges, or Ganga, is a river in India that is considered a manifestation of the Goddess in the Hindu tradition.

OCTOBER

OCTOBER 1

Each soul's attainment
Is according to its evolution.

OCTOBER 2

It always means that you must sacrifice
Something very dear to you
When God's call comes.

OCTOBER 3

Renunciation

Is always for a purpose;

It is to kindle the soul

That nothing may hold it back from God;

But when it is kindled, the life of renunciation

Is not necessary.

OCTOBER 4

There are those who are like a lighted candle:

They can light other candles,

But the other candles

Must be of wax—

If they are of steel,

They cannot be lighted.

OCTOBER 5

There is no greater scripture than Nature,
For Nature is life itself.

OCTOBER 6

Wisdom can only be learned gradually,
And every soul is not ready to receive
Or to understand the complexity
Of the purpose of life.

OCTOBER 7

It is a very high stage on the path of love
When one really learns to love another
With a love that asks no return.

OCTOBER 8

Love alone
Is the fountain
From which all virtues fall
As drops of sparkling water.

OCTOBER 9

The whole purpose of life
Is to make God a reality.

OCTOBER 10

If you seek the good
In every soul, you will always find it,
For God is in all things.
Still more, God is in all beings.

OCTOBER 11

The knowledge of God
Is beyond Humanity's reason.
The secret of God
Is hidden in the knowledge of unity.

OCTOBER 12

Seek God in all souls,
Good or bad, wise or foolish,
Attractive and unattractive;
In the depths of each there is God.

OCTOBER 13

When in ourselves
There is disharmony,
How can we spread harmony?

OCTOBER 14

The inmost being of a human
Is the real being of God.

OCTOBER 15

Love itself
Is the healing power
And the remedy for all pain.

OCTOBER 16

By loving, forgiving and serving,
It is possible for your whole life to become
One single vision of the sublime beauty of God.

OCTOBER 17

Mysticism
To the mystic
Is both science and religion.

OCTOBER 18

The principles of mysticism
Rise from the heart of the human being;
They are learned by intuition and proved by reason.

OCTOBER 19

Your work in life
Must be your religion,
Whatever your occupation be.

OCTOBER 20

The true joy of every soul
Is in the realization of the Divine Spirit,
And the absence of realization
Keeps the soul in despair.

OCTOBER 21

Beyond the narrow barriers of race and creed
We can all unite, because
We all belong to one God.

OCTOBER 22

All forms of worship or prayer
Draw one closer to God.

OCTOBER 23

When one is separated from God in thought,
Belief is of no use, worship is of little use.

OCTOBER 24

The source of the realization of truth is within;
One's Self is the object of realization.

OCTOBER 25

True self-denial
Is losing one's self in God.

OCTOBER 26

It is more important
To find out the truth about one's Self
Than to find out the truth of Heaven and Hell.

OCTOBER 27

According to one's evolution,
One knows the truth; and the more one knows,
The more one finds there is to know.

OCTOBER 28

The person filled with the knowledge
Of names and forms
Has no capacity for the knowledge of truth.

OCTOBER 29

One mistakes
When one begins to cultivate the heart
By wanting to sow the seed oneself
Instead of leaving the sowing
To God.

OCTOBER 30

Friends, we start our lives as teachers,
And it is very hard for us to learn to become pupils.
There are many whose only difficulty in life
Is that they are teachers already.
What we have to learn is discipleship.
There is but one teacher,
God.

OCTOBER 31

Earthly knowledge

Is as clouds dimming the sight,

And it is the breaking of these clouds—

In other words, purity of heart—

That gives the capacity

For the knowledge

Of God

To rise.

NOVEMBER

NOVEMBER 1

The self stands as a wall
Between us and God.

NOVEMBER 2

It is a patient pursuit to bring water
From the depth of the ground;
One has to deal with much mud
In digging before one reaches
The water of life.

NOVEMBER 3

In one's search for truth,

The first and last lesson is love.

There must be no separation.

No "I am" and "you are not."

Until one has arrived at that selfless consciousness,

One cannot know life and truth.

NOVEMBER 4

By the power of prayer,

One opens the door of the heart,

In which God, the ever-forgiving,

The all merciful, abides.

NOVEMBER 5

To be really sorry for one's errors

Is like opening the doors of Heaven.

NOVEMBER 6

Our soul is blessed
With the impression of the glory of God
Whenever we praise God.

NOVEMBER 7

As a child learning to walk
Falls a thousand times
Before it can stand,
And after that, falls again and again,
Until at last it can walk,
So are we as little children before God.

NOVEMBER 8

Self-denial is not renouncing things,
It is denying the self;
And the first lesson of self-denial
Is humility.

NOVEMBER 9

The more elevated the soul,
The broader the outlook.

NOVEMBER 10

Mastery lies not merely in stilling the mind,
But in directing it toward whatever point you desire.

NOVEMBER 11

Our thoughts have prepared for us
The happiness or unhappiness we experience.

NOVEMBER 12

When the mind and body are restless,
Nothing in life can be accomplished.
Success is the result of control.

NOVEMBER 13

When speech is controlled, the eyes speak;
The glance says what words can never say.

NOVEMBER 14

Words are but shells
Of thoughts and feelings.

NOVEMBER 15

Wisdom is not in words;
It is in understanding.

NOVEMBER 16

The Message of God
Is like a spring of water—it rises and falls
And makes its way by itself.

NOVEMBER 17

If the eyes and ears are open,

The leaves of the trees become

As pages of the Bible.*

NOVEMBER 18

The soul of all is one soul,

And the truth is one truth,

Under whatever religion it is hidden.

NOVEMBER 19

Narrowness is not necessarily devotion

But often appears so.

---

* In Hazrat Pir-o-Murshid Inayat Khan's "Ten Sufi Thoughts," he says: "There is one Holy Book, the sacred manuscript of nature, the only scripture which can enlighten the reader."

NOVEMBER 20

It is the soul's light
That is the natural intelligence.

NOVEMBER 21

The wave is the sea itself;
Yet when it rises in the form of a wave,
It is the wave,
And when you look at the whole of it,
It is the sea.

NOVEMBER 22

It is not the solid wood that can become a flute,
It is the empty reed.*

---

* The *ney*, a reed-pipe, or flute blown from the end is a traditional instrument of Sufi music.

NOVEMBER 23

Reason is learned from the ever-changing world,
But true knowledge comes from the essence of life.

NOVEMBER 24

God is within you.
You are God's instrument
And through you God expresses God's Self
To the external world.

NOVEMBER 25

It is according to the extent
Of our consciousness in prayer
That our prayer reaches God.

NOVEMBER 26

The heart must be empty
In order to receive the knowledge of God.

NOVEMBER 27

As long as in love
There is "you" and "me,"
Love is not fully kindled.

NOVEMBER 28

Once you have given up
Your limited self willingly to the Unlimited,
You will rejoice so much in that consciousness
That you will not care to be small again.

NOVEMBER 29

The deeper your prayers echo
In your own consciousness,
The more audible they are to God.

NOVEMBER 30

It is the depth of thought that is powerful,
And sincerity of feeling that creates atmosphere.

DECEMBER

DECEMBER 1

The higher you rise,
The wider becomes the margin of your view.

DECEMBER 2

Justice can never be developed
While we judge others.
The only way is by constantly judging ourselves.

DECEMBER 3

Joy and sorrow
Are the light and shade of life.
Without light and shade no picture is clear.

DECEMBER 4

The wise one
Submits to conditions when helpless,
Bowing to the will of God.
But the sin that is avoidable
One roots out without sparing
A single moment or effort.

DECEMBER 5

Enviable is one who loves
And asks no return.

DECEMBER 6

To deny the changeableness of life
Is like fancying a motionless sea,
Which can only exist in one's imagination.

DECEMBER 7

Learn to live a true life
And you will know the truth.

DECEMBER 8

Wisdom is attained
In solitude.

DECEMBER 9

The seeming death of the body
Is the real birth of the soul.

DECEMBER 10

As the rose blooms amidst thorns,
So great souls shine out through all opposition.

DECEMBER 11

When the artist loses the self in the art,
Then the art comes to life.

DECEMBER 12

Do not anything with fear;
And fear not whatever you do.

DECEMBER 13

Love develops into harmony,
And of harmony is born beauty.

DECEMBER 14

One who keeps no secrets
Has no depth in the heart.

DECEMBER 15

Behind us all is one spirit and one life;
How then can we be happy if our neighbor
Is not also happy?

DECEMBER 16

The sea of life is in constant motion,
No one can stop its ever-moving waves.
The master walks over the waves,
The wise one swims in the water,
But the ignorant one is drowned
In the effort to cross.

DECEMBER 17

The human being's greatest privilege
Is to become a suitable instrument of God.

DECEMBER 18

The trees of the forest
Silently await God's blessing.

DECEMBER 19

The plain truth
Is too simple for the seeker after complexity
Who is looking for things they cannot understand.

DECEMBER 20

An unsuccessful person often keeps success away
By the impression of their former failures.

DECEMBER 21

The human being is the tree of desire,
And the root of that tree is in our own heart.

DECEMBER 22

With good-will and trust in God,
Self-confidence and a hopeful attitude toward life,
One can always win the battle,
However difficult.

DECEMBER 23

There are many paths,
And everyone considers their own
The best and wisest.
Let everyone choose that which
Belongs to their own temperament.

DECEMBER 24

Failure, either in health or affairs,
Means there has been lack of self-control.

DECEMBER 25

Love is as the water of the Ganges;*
It is in itself a purification.

DECEMBER 26

Love is unlimited,
But it needs scope to expand and rise;
Without that scope
Life is unhappy.

---

* The Ganges, or Ganga, is a river in India that is considered a
manifestation of the Goddess in the Hindu tradition.

DECEMBER 27

Every wave of the sea, as it rises,

Seems to be stretching its hands upwards,

As if to say, "take me higher and higher."

DECEMBER 28

True pleasure

Lies in the sharing of joy with another.

DECEMBER 29

A gain or loss that is momentary is not real;

If we knew realities,

We should never grieve over the loss of anything

Which experience shows to be only transitory.

DECEMBER 30

A soul is as great
As the circle of its influence.

DECEMBER 31

Happiness lies in thinking or doing
That which one considers beautiful.

HAZRAT INAYAT KHAN was born in India in 1882. A master of Indian classical music, he gave up a brilliant career as a musician to devote himself full-time to the spiritual path. In 1910, he was sent into the West by his spiritual teacher and began to teach Sufism in the United States, England, and throughout Europe. For a decade and a half he traveled tirelessly, giving lectures and guiding an ever-growing group of Western spiritual seekers. In 1926, he returned to India and died there the following year. Today, his universalist Sufi teachings continue to inspire countless people around the world and his spiritual heirs may be found in every corner of the planet.